LOVE AND BEYOND

TRUE TALES OF ROMANCE

WESLEY L. DIENER

TABLE OF CONTENTS

INTRODUCTION

Exploring the Realm of Romance

Love, in all its beautiful and complex forms, is a force that transcends time, culture, and circumstance. It's the universal language of the heart, the subject of countless poems, songs, and stories. In this journey through the pages of "Love and Beyond: True Tales of Romance," we embark on an exploration of the boundless dimensions of love.

The realm of romance is a tapestry woven with threads of passion, connection, and human experience. It's a world where the ordinary becomes extraordinary, where chance encounters lead to profound connections, and where love triumphs over adversity. It's a realm where cultural differences blend seamlessly, where friendship blossoms into something deeper, and where love defies conventions.

Within these chapters, you will find a collection of true stories, each a testament to the enduring power of love. These are not merely accounts of fleeting moments but chronicles of love's resilience, its capacity to inspire, and its ability to transform lives. They are stories of real people, each with a unique narrative, bound by a common thread—their profound experience of love.

As we delve into these tales, we will unravel the intricacies of love and its profound impact on our lives. We will discover that love knows no boundaries, that it can weather life's storms, and that it has the remarkable ability to heal and uplift. Most importantly, we will gain insights and wisdom from these stories, lessons that we can carry with us as we navigate our own journeys in the realm of romance.

So, dear reader, let us embark on this voyage together, as we explore the depths of love and beyond. These true tales of romance are not just stories; they are windows into the human heart, and within them, you may find echoes of your own experiences, hopes, and dreams. Welcome to the enchanting world of "Love and Beyond," where the power of love knows no bounds.

CHAPTER 1: LOVE ACROSS TIME AND DISTANCE

Long-Distance Love Stories

Long-distance love is a phenomenon of our interconnected world, where individuals can form deep and meaningful connections with someone thousands of miles away. It's a paradox where physical distance challenges the strength of emotional bonds. In this section, we explore the complexities and beauty of long-distance love.

For many, the journey of a long-distance relationship starts with a leap of faith. It's a decision to invest time, energy, and emotions into a connection that defies geographical boundaries. But it's also a testament to the power of love in the digital age. Through social media, video calls, and messaging apps, couples can stay connected, share experiences, and create memories, even when they can't be physically present with each other.

In long-distance relationships, communication is the lifeline that keeps the connection alive. Couples find creative ways to bridge the gap and maintain intimacy. They write heartfelt letters, send surprise care packages, and plan virtual date nights where they can share a meal or watch a movie together, despite being miles apart.

What makes long-distance love truly remarkable is the depth of emotional connection that can develop when physical closeness is not an option. Couples often find themselves communicating more openly and honestly, building a foundation of trust and emotional intimacy.

Long-distance love isn't without its challenges. Trust issues, jealousy, and the longing for physical presence can put strain on even the strongest bonds. However, many couples find ways to turn these challenges into opportunities for growth.

They learn the art of trust, communicate openly about their feelings, and build a strong foundation of emotional support. Some even view the time spent apart as a chance for personal growth and self-discovery, making them more appreciative of their partner when they reunite.

Ageless Romances

Ageless romances, where love transcends generational gaps, challenge societal norms and stereotypes. Love doesn't always adhere to age boundaries, and in this section, we explore the dynamics of relationships with significant age differences.

These relationships often carry unique dynamics, with partners coming from different life stages and bringing diverse perspectives. But at their core, they are driven by genuine love and connection that defy age-related expectations.

Age can bring depth and wisdom to romantic relationships. In ageless romances, partners may benefit from each other's life experiences. Older individuals may provide guidance and support, while younger partners can infuse new energy and perspectives into the relationship.

These relationships are not solely about the age difference but about the mutual respect, understanding, and love that transcends the numbers on a birth certificate.

Some love stories have the power to span

generations, leaving a lasting legacy of love within families. These are tales of love that grandparents, parents, and children cherish and pass down through the ages.

The significance of these stories lies not just in the romantic aspect but in the enduring commitment and connection they represent. They remind us that love can be a bond that ties generations together, enriching the family tapestry with stories of enduring love.

CHAPTER 2 : UNEXPECTED ENCOUNTERS AND CHANCE MEETINGS

In the vast tapestry of love stories, some of the most captivating tales emerge from the realm of serendipity. These are the stories where fate takes the reins, orchestrating encounters that change lives forever. In this chapter, we delve into serendipitous love stories and explore how love can blossom in the most unlikely places.

Serendipitous Love Stories

The Coffee Shop Connection: In a bustling city, two strangers with vastly different lives cross paths at a cozy coffee shop. Their chance meeting over spilled coffee leads to an unexpected romance that defies all odds.

The Lost and Found Love: A misplaced item at a crowded event brought two souls together. What starts as a frantic search turns into a serendipitous love story of finding each other in the most unexpected way.

Amidst the hustle and bustle of a vibrant summer festival, Emily and Michael found themselves unwittingly intertwined by the whims of fate. Emily had been browsing through colorful stalls, her heart set on finding the perfect handcrafted necklace. Michael, on the other hand, was navigating the lively crowd with his friends, enjoying the energetic atmosphere of the event. Their paths collided when Emily's treasured pendant slipped from her grasp, disappearing into the sea of festival-goers.

Panic set in as Emily frantically searched for her lost necklace, tears of frustration welling up in her eyes. It was then that Michael, noticing her distress, extended a helping hand. With kind eyes and a comforting smile, he joined the quest to recover her beloved pendant. As they scoured the bustling festival grounds together, their initial frantic search transformed into moments of shared laughter, exchanged stories, and stolen glances. Little did they know that the lost necklace would lead them to find something far more precious – an unexpected love that blossomed amidst the chaos of that crowded event.

Love in Unlikely Places

The Library Romance: For book lovers, the library is a sanctuary of knowledge, but for these two individuals, it becomes the backdrop for a love story filled with shared interests and whispered conversations among the bookshelves.

A Culinary Connection: Sometimes, love is found in the most unexpected dishes. Explore how a chance encounter in a cooking class ignited a passionate flame between two aspiring chefs.

In a cozy little cooking class tucked away in the heart of the city, two aspiring chefs, Alex and Mia, had a chance encounter that would change their lives forever. They both signed up for the class with different intentions—Alex, to finally learn how to cook beyond instant noodles, and Mia, to conquer her fear of open flames. Fate, however, had other plans. As they fumbled with knives and giggled over spilled ingredients, their initial awkwardness slowly turned into a shared passion for the culinary arts.

With each passing class, Alex and Mia found themselves eagerly anticipating their weekly cooking adventures. They discovered that their tastes and techniques complemented each other perfectly, creating dishes that were nothing short of magical. The kitchen became their playground, where they danced between sizzling pans and bubbling pots, their laughter and connection filling the room. As they perfected recipes and created their own unique dishes, they realized that love, much like cooking, was all about the right ingredients coming together at the perfect moment.

The Art Gallery Affection: In the quiet corridors of an art gallery, a chance encounter sparks a deep connection between a pair of art enthusiasts. Their shared appreciation for creativity transcends the boundaries of a typical romance.

These stories are just a glimpse into the enchanting world of serendipitous love and the uncharted territories of romance found in unexpected places. They remind us that love has a way of defying logic and embracing the unpredictable. Join us on a journey through these heartwarming tales of love that bloomed from the most unexpected encounters.

CHAPTER 3: LOVE TRIUMPHS OVER ADVERSITY

Love isn't always smooth sailing. In fact, some of the most beautiful love stories are the ones that faced tough challenges and came out stronger. In this chapter, we'll explore how love can overcome obstacles and adversity.

Overcoming Challenges in Love

Love is a powerful force, but it doesn't mean everything will be easy. In fact, many couples encounter hurdles along the way. These challenges can be anything from misunderstandings to external pressures like family or work. It's crucial to remember that facing these challenges together can strengthen your bond. Let's look at some values that can sustain us when our love faces stories.

Communication is Key: One of the most common challenges in love is miscommunication. Open and honest communication is paramount in resolving issues between lovers as it fosters trust, understanding, and emotional connection.

When partners openly express their feelings, concerns, and needs, it creates a safe space for vulnerability and empathy. This transparency allows them to address misunderstandings, work through conflicts, and find mutually satisfying solutions. By actively listening and sharing their thoughts without judgment, lovers can build a stronger foundation of intimacy, ultimately strengthening their relationship and ensuring that issues are addressed constructively rather than festering into larger problems.

Resilience in Love: When life throws curveballs, love can be a source of strength.

Sarah and Mark were deeply in love, but their relationship faced an unexpected challenge when Mark was diagnosed with a serious health condition. At first, the news was overwhelming, and fear threatened to overshadow their connection. However, instead of retreating, Sarah and Mark chose to confront the situation head-on. They began attending doctor's appointments together, researching treatment options, and openly discussing their fears and hopes. Through this process, they discovered a new level of emotional support and resilience. Their love became a source of strength, motivating Mark to stay positive and fight his illness with unwavering determination. Sarah, in turn, found strength in her role as Mark's pillar of support. Their love not only endured but grew stronger as they faced health troubles together, demonstrating the incredible power of love in the face of adversity.

As Mark's treatment progressed, they cherished every moment together, focusing on making precious memories and appreciating the beauty of life. Their shared experiences brought them closer, and they learned to appreciate the simple joys in each other's company. This journey of facing health troubles allowed Sarah and Mark to redefine the meaning of love and resilience. Their unwavering commitment to one another and their ability to find strength in adversity served as an inspiring example of how love can conquer even the most formidable challenges life may throw their way.

Love in the Face of Life's Obstacles

Life can be unpredictable, but love can be a constant. Let's explore how love can shine even when faced with life's biggest obstacles.

Sometimes, families or cultural backgrounds can create challenges for couples. Love has a remarkable ability to transcend the barriers that families or cultural backgrounds may inadvertently impose on lovers. Often, these challenges stem from differing values, traditions, or expectations held by each person's respective family or cultural community. However, when two individuals deeply care for one another, their love becomes a unifying force that can bridge these gaps. It fosters understanding and tolerance, encouraging couples to find common ground, even amid contrasting backgrounds. Love empowers individuals to engage in open, empathetic conversations with their families and to educate them about the importance of their relationship, ultimately leading to acceptance and support. This process of love's transformational power allows couples to overcome initial obstacles and create a harmonious union that celebrates both their shared love and their unique cultural backgrounds.

In addition to fostering understanding and unity,

love often serves as a catalyst for personal growth and adaptation. When two people from different cultural backgrounds come together, they learn to appreciate and respect each other's traditions and values. This exchange enriches their own perspectives and helps them evolve into more open-minded individuals. Moreover, love encourages couples to create their own unique blend of traditions and values, thereby forging a new cultural identity that combines the best of both worlds. Through this process, love not only bridges the gaps between families and cultural backgrounds but also creates a tapestry of diversity that enriches the relationship and contributes positively to society's broader cultural landscape. Love's transformative power, therefore, goes beyond merely bringing two people together; it also helps them create a more inclusive and harmonious world.

Moreover, distance indeed presents a substantial obstacle in modern relationships. In today's interconnected world, individuals often find themselves in situations where geographical separation becomes a defining factor in their love lives. The challenges of maintaining a strong emotional connection, trust, and communication can be daunting when partners are physically distant. The absence of face-to-face interaction can lead to feelings of loneliness and insecurity, as couples must rely heavily on virtual means to stay connected. Overcoming these hurdles often requires a high level of commitment, dedication, and the ability to adapt to the unique dynamics of long-distance relationships.

Despite the obstacles, distance can also serve as a test of a relationship's strength and resilience. When couples successfully navigate the challenges of being apart, it can deepen their bond and strengthen their connection. The effort put into maintaining communication, trust, and intimacy despite the miles can lead to a greater appreciation for each other and a sense of accomplishment. Moreover, distance can offer individuals an opportunity for personal growth and independence, allowing them to pursue their own goals and aspirations while still nurturing their love. In this way, while distance can be a formidable challenge, it can also be a crucible that forges enduring and profound relationships for those who are willing to invest the time and effort required to bridge the physical gap.

Love isn't always smooth sailing. In fact, some of the most beautiful love stories are the ones that faced tough challenges and came out stronger. In overcoming challenges, trust plays a vital role. Lovers who love each other without trust may not last long in their relationship. This means that they don't know and understand each other because it's who you know and understand that you can trust.

Lovers should act fast on discovering each other's propensities. This is a sure way to build trust in others. There may be hearsays but because we know the abilities and capabilities of our partners, we can easily identify when outsiders want to intrude into and spoil our love lives.

CHAPTER 4: LOVE AND CULTURE

Cross-Cultural Romances

In the intricate tapestry of human relationships, cross-cultural romances stand out as threads woven from diverse backgrounds, creating a unique and colorful pattern of love. These unions, often born from chance meetings, online connections, or shared experiences, come with their own set of challenges and rewards. As a marriage counselor and couples therapist, I have witnessed firsthand the beauty and complexities that cross-cultural couples bring to their relationships.

It's no secret that all relationships come with their share of challenges and opportunities for growth. However, cross-cultural couples may find themselves seeking online couples therapy or relationship coaching because they face unique hurdles in bridging the gap between their diverse backgrounds. The reasons are understandable: there's often much to work through, and it can be easy to fall into a power struggle when each partner feels strongly that their way of being is "correct."

Cross-cultural relationships or intercultural couples can have vastly different relationship expectations. These differences may extend to gender roles in the home, the role of extended family, communication styles, and much more. While the diversity of their union can ultimately lead to an enormously strong and healthy relationship, it's not uncommon for couples from very different cultural or racial backgrounds to need to put in extra effort to create understanding and compromise in order to connect with each other.

It's crucial to note that everyone enters a relationship from a unique family of origin background, each with its own values, belief systems, internal culture, and way of doing things. Even individuals who may seem, on the surface, to be of similar backgrounds may have had entirely different "family cultures" that influence their expectations in their relationship with their partner. These differences can create resentment when expectations go unmet.

This underlying issue is often the reason why financial therapy for couples becomes necessary. The values and expectations instilled by one's family of origin can profoundly impact how a person views money and financial decisions within a relationship.

One of the significant strengths of interracial couples, cross-cultural couples, and international couples is their overt awareness of the need to openly discuss and respect these differences to achieve congruence. "Constructive conflict" becomes a non-negotiable relationship skill for most couples, especially those coming from very different places and perspectives. In contrast, couples who assume that their partner's life experiences were similar to their own run the risk of having unspoken assumptions and expectations lead to conflict, emotional turmoil, and hurt feelings.

From the outset, understanding that both partners have perspectives, values, and expectations that are simultaneously different and equally valuable becomes a significant asset. This realization forms the foundation for fruitful dialogue, compromise, and mutual growth.

Love Beyond Borders

In the realm of cross-cultural romances, love

knows no boundaries. It is the force that brings together individuals from different corners of the world, transcending geographical, cultural, and linguistic divides. These relationships are a testament to the boundless nature of human connection, where two souls, often separated by thousands of miles, find each other in the vast expanse of the Internet or through serendipitous encounters.

Cross-cultural romances are characterized by their ability to forge connections that defy traditional limitations. In an era of globalization and digital interconnectedness, love has the power to bridge geographical gaps. Online dating platforms and social media have become modern Cupids, introducing individuals who might never have met otherwise.

The allure of these relationships lies in the excitement of exploring a different world through the eyes of a loved one. Partners from diverse backgrounds bring their unique experiences, traditions, and perspectives to the relationship, enriching each other's lives in the process.

However, love beyond borders is not without its

challenges. The physical separation that often accompanies cross-cultural relationships can be daunting. Couples must navigate time zones, visa requirements, and the yearning for in-person connections. The longing to be together can be both a test of patience and a testament to the strength of their love.

Additionally, cultural differences can lead to misunderstandings. What may be considered a romantic gesture in one culture might be seen differently in another. These disparities in expectations and norms can create moments of confusion, requiring open communication and a willingness to learn from one another.

Despite these challenges, cross-cultural couples often discover the universal truth that love transcends cultural boundaries. It reminds us that, at our core, we share the same fundamental desires for companionship, understanding, and connection. Love becomes the common language that allows partners to navigate the complexities of merging two worlds into one.

CHAPTER 5: LOVE AND FRIENDSHIP

When Friends Become Lovers

You've likely heard the age-old adage that a solid friendship forms the bedrock of any lasting romantic relationship. The notion of viewing your partner as your best friend, your confidant, your go-to person, is often heralded as a recipe for a successful long-term relationship or marriage.

However, the question often arises: Should the friendship come first, or should attraction precede friendship and then evolve alongside it? Is there a specific order to follow, or are there discernible signs that friendship is on the cusp of blossoming into love? Can you genuinely be friends before becoming lovers, and if so, how does this transformation occur?

The truth is, it can unfold in various ways. Sometimes, you might feel an immediate attraction and a desire for a romantic relationship from the outset. Conversely, you may find yourself becoming attracted to someone you've known as a friend, gradually recognizing the signs that your friendship is turning into love.

Yet, let's be honest, the latter scenario can be an intricate and bewildering journey. When your platonic feelings unexpectedly transform into romantic emotions for a close friend, it can feel like uncharted territory. It often prompts a flood of questions: "Are we more than friends now?", "Can a friendship truly transition into a successful romantic relationship?", "What happens if the romantic aspect doesn't endure?"

So, what does it mean when we say a friendship is turning into love? When that transformation takes place, it's akin to a spark igniting within. Suddenly, you find yourself caring more deeply, experiencing delightful butterflies in your stomach, and realizing that their smile has become your personal sunshine. It's a beautiful voyage, progressing from merely knowing each other to understanding each other's hearts.

Nonetheless, this journey from friendship to love can indeed be complex. Feelings may surface unexpectedly, and the fear of jeopardizing a cherished friendship can cast a shadow of doubt and insecurity, making the path seem even more challenging.

But here's the crux of it: Is it genuinely possible for a friendship to evolve into love? Can friends become lovers, or are these just romantic ideals? These are the questions that undoubtedly occupy your mind, and perhaps even your friend's.

The truth is, if you've developed strong romantic feelings for someone who is already your friend, it's actually a positive circumstance. Why, you ask? Well, because a close friendship lays a firm foundation for a romantic relationship. Consider it this way: you already know this person quite well. You've recognized their admirable qualities (which might be why you've developed feelings in the first place), and you're acquainted with their flaws, just as they are with yours.

This knowledge and acceptance of each other's authentic selves can make the initial phase of infatuation and attraction in the relationship smoother. You don't feel compelled to present only your best selves because you're comfortable being your true selves around each other. In essence, it's entirely plausible for a friendship to precede a romantic relationship. Falling in love with your best friend can indeed be a reality.

However, there's a crucial caveat: Does your friend reciprocate these romantic feelings? Do they desire a romantic relationship with you? This is where the signs come into play, the indicators that a friendship is teetering on the brink of becoming something more. But before we delve into those signs, let's explore the critical aspects to consider in the next section.

Here are 10 signs that a friendship is evolving into a deeper affection, transitioning from being friends to potentially becoming lovers:

1. **Increased Communication:** You notice that the frequency of your communication has significantly increased. You're texting, calling, and talking more often than before. This heightened connection indicates a shift in your relationship dynamics.

2. **Jealousy and Protectiveness:** You find yourself experiencing jealousy when your friend talks about their ex-partners or potential

romantic interests. The thought of them being with someone else makes you uncomfortable, a clear sign of developing deeper feelings.

3. **Evolved Body Language:** Pay attention to your body language when you're together. Subtle cues, like sitting or standing closer, touching more often, or feeling more comfortable with physical contact, suggest that your connection is transitioning from platonic to romantic.

4. **Emotional Intimacy:** You begin sharing deeper, more personal thoughts and feelings with your friend. This emotional intimacy goes beyond typical friendship, as you both open up in ways you haven't before.

5. **Quality Time Together:** You find yourselves spending more quality time together, seeking out activities that involve just the two of you. This could include movie nights, dinners, or outings that feel like "date" activities.

6. **Flirting and Teasing:** Playful flirting and teasing become more prominent in your interactions. Light teasing, compliments, and subtle hints of attraction start to emerge in your conversations.

7. **Interest in Their Life:** You take a keen interest in their life, including their dreams, aspirations, and personal growth. This deeper curiosity about their well-being goes beyond the typical concern of a friend.

8. **Dreams and Future Planning:** You both begin discussing your future plans and goals together. Conversations about where you see yourselves in the future often include each other in significant ways.

9. **Support and Encouragement:** You offer unwavering support and encouragement for their endeavors, even if it means making personal sacrifices. Your dedication to their success is indicative of your deeper emotional investment.

10. **Shared Long-Term Vision:** Both of you start envisioning a future together, whether it's discussing potential vacations, moving in together, or considering the possibility of a long-term romantic commitment. These conversations reveal your shared aspirations for a deeper connection.

These signs collectively indicate a transition from friendship to a more romantic affection.

However, it's essential to communicate openly with your friend about these feelings to ensure mutual understanding and consent before moving forward with a romantic relationship.

CHAPTER 6: UNCONVENTIONAL LOVE STRATEGIES

In the realm of romance, unconventional love strategies often provide the most memorable and heartwarming tales. These stories are not about following the well-trodden path of dating norms or societal expectations. Instead, they celebrate the uniqueness of each love story, highlighting the profound connections that can emerge from unorthodox approaches. Take, for instance, the couple who embarked on a spontaneous road trip together, barely knowing each other, and found love blossoming along the winding roads and unexpected detours. Or the person who wrote love letters to their future partner for years, keeping them in a secret box until the day they finally met. Unconventional love strategies are a testament to the creative and sometimes daring ways people navigate the winding paths of love, reminding us that the heart is a boundless explorer.

Unique Paths to Love

Love, as it turns out, is a master of unpredictability. Some of the most beautiful and enduring love stories have emerged from the most unexpected beginnings. These tales celebrate the whimsical nature of fate, revealing that love knows no boundaries or conventions. Imagine the couple who met during a delayed flight, bonding over shared travel woes and discovering a deep connection that led to a lifetime of adventures together. Or the pair who initially disliked each other but found love blossoming when they were forced to collaborate on a project. These unique paths to love highlight that the heart's journey is often filled with delightful surprises, and love can flourish in the most unlikely places. They remind us that the magic of love is often found in the unscripted moments of our lives.

Unique paths to love can vary widely, but some of the more common ones involve unexpected encounters or circumstances that lead to profound connections. Here are a few of the most common unique paths to love:

1. **Chance Meetings:** Meeting someone unexpectedly in a place you wouldn't typically frequent, like a coffee shop, airport, or even on public transportation, can lead to a unique and memorable love story.

2. **Shared Hobbies or Interests:** Bonding over a shared passion or hobby, whether it's a love for books, sports, music, or a particular activity, can bring people together in unexpected ways.

3. **Mutual Friends:** Sometimes, love blooms when introduced to someone through mutual friends or acquaintances. This can lead to unexpected connections with people you might not have met otherwise.

4. **Volunteer or Charity Work:** Collaborating on a volunteer project or working together for a charitable cause can create a deep sense of connection and shared purpose, often leading to romantic relationships.

5. **Online Dating:** While online dating is becoming more common, the way people meet and connect online can still be quite unique. The Internet allows individuals from different geographical locations and backgrounds to find love.

6. **Travel Adventures:** Traveling, especially solo travel, can lead to unique encounters with people from different cultures and backgrounds. These connections can sometimes evolve into deep and meaningful

romances.

7. **Workplace Romances:** While not uncommon, falling in love with a coworker can still be considered a unique path to romance, as it often involves navigating the complexities of a professional setting.

8. **Unlikely Circumstances:** Love can also emerge from challenging or unexpected situations, such as overcoming a shared crisis or experiencing personal growth together.

9. **Reconnecting with Old Friends:** Reconnecting with an old friend or childhood acquaintance after many years can lead to the rekindling of a deeper connection and the discovery of romantic feelings.

10. **Arranged Marriages:** In some cultures, arranged marriages can be considered unique by modern Western standards. These marriages are based on the compatibility of families and values, and love often grows over time.

These are just a few examples of the many unique paths to love that people have experienced. Each love story is special and often characterized by the unexpected nature of how two individuals come together.

Love in Unexpected Forms

In the world of romance, love often takes on unexpected and beautiful forms. It can be profound, yet subtle; it can challenge our preconceived notions while leaving us in awe of its transformative power. Love between people of different generations, where wisdom meets youthful enthusiasm, creates a unique and nurturing bond. Love that transcends language barriers, relying on shared glances and gestures, showcases the universality of human connection. Even love for a hobby or shared interest can be a powerful force, bringing people together in unexpected ways. These tales of love in unexpected forms reveal that the heart is a versatile canvas where countless unique expressions of love can be painted. They teach us that love is not confined to a single mold but flourishes in countless beautiful and surprising ways, enriching our lives with its diverse forms.

Love has a remarkable ability to transcend conventional boundaries, often manifesting itself in the most unexpected and beautiful forms. This unique aspect of love is a testament to its boundless nature and the human capacity for connection. "Love in Unexpected Forms" explores the fascinating world of love stories that defy traditional norms and expectations, shining a light on the diverse expressions of affection that exist in our lives.

One of the most captivating aspects of love in unexpected forms is the way it challenges preconceived notions. In our journey through life, we often imagine love to be a well-defined emotion, but it surprises us when it takes on shapes we didn't anticipate. Take, for example, the deep bond that forms between people of different generations. This unique interplay of wisdom and youthful enthusiasm creates a love that's nurturing and transformative, showing that love knows no age or bounds. It reminds us that in the world of relationships, age is merely a number, and the heart knows its own desires.

Language barriers, too, can become a canvas for unexpected love to flourish. Love stories that emerge between individuals who don't share a common language showcase the power of non-verbal communication. These couples rely on shared glances, gestures, and expressions to convey their feelings, revealing that love transcends words. This form of love illustrates that human connection is a universal language, unbound by linguistic boundaries.

Furthermore, love can take shape in the shared appreciation of hobbies or interests. When two individuals come together over a mutual passion, whether it's art, sports, music, or a unique hobby, a unique and profound connection forms. These relationships often thrive because they are rooted in shared values, experiences, and interests, demonstrating that love can emerge from the most unexpected sources of commonality.

In essence, "Love in Unexpected Forms" celebrates the versatility of the human heart. It teaches us that love is not confined to a single mold or predetermined path. Instead, it flourishes in countless beautiful and surprising ways, enriching our lives with its diverse expressions. These tales of love in unexpected forms inspire us to be open to the unexpected, to embrace the unique, and to recognize that love, in all its forms, is a force that connects us in the most extraordinary ways.

CHAPTER 7: LESSONS FROM TRUE TALES OF ROMANCE

As we finish our journey through the stories in "Love and Beyond: True Tales of Romance," we've learned a lot about love and how it works in real life. We saw love stories that happened when people met by chance or when they faced tough times together. Now, it's time to talk about what we can learn from these stories and how love affects our lives.

Insights and Takeaways

1. Love Can Be Tough: We discovered that love isn't always easy. In these stories, love faced challenges, but it stayed strong. This shows us that love can endure difficulties and become even stronger because of them.

2. Surprise Love: Many of these stories began with unexpected meetings. Love can happen when we least expect it. Being open to surprises can lead to wonderful love stories.

3. Talk to Each Other: Good communication is super important in love. It means sharing your feelings honestly and really listening when your partner talks. When couples talk openly and respectfully, their love tends to last.

4. Love Knows No Limits: These stories crossed all kinds of boundaries like culture, distance, and rules. Love has this amazing ability to bring people together, no matter where they come from.

5. Friendship Counts: We saw that being good friends first can lead to deeper love. Building a strong friendship with your partner can make your love even better.

How Love Changes Our Lives

Love isn't just a feeling; it's a big part of who we are. It inspires us to be kinder, braver, and more caring. Love makes us want to take chances and support each other. It influences the choices we make, what matters most to us, and what we dream about.

Love teaches us important stuff like patience, forgiveness, and how to work things out when we don't agree. It challenges us to grow and become better people, both on our own and as a couple. Love reminds us that we're all connected, and everyone wants to feel loved and belong somewhere.

In the end, the love stories in this book are like mirrors reflecting different sides of love in our world. They remind us that no matter who we are or where we're from, love can be a powerful force in our lives. These stories aren't just tales; they're like guides, showing us the way love works.

We're ending this journey here, but your own love story is still being written. Remember what we've learned: Love can be tough, surprising, and it's all about understanding each other. Let these lessons be your guide as you keep exploring the exciting world of love and relationships. Your own love story is waiting to be told, and it might be the most beautiful one yet.

CONCLUSION: CELEBRATING THE WONDERS OF LOVE

In wrapping up our journey through these real tales of romance, let's take a moment to savor the remarkable beauty of love.

Love is an extraordinary force that knows no boundaries. It's not just something we see in movies or read about in books. It's alive in the stories we've explored, where ordinary people like you and me found something truly extraordinary. These tales remind us that love is not confined by time or distance. It has the power to bridge gaps, whether they be miles, years, or even cultural divides.

Think about those moments when love unexpectedly taps us on the shoulder, when we meet someone who becomes an integral part of our lives. Those chance encounters, the spark that ignites when we least expect it — that's the magic of love. It's the thrilling serendipity that can make our hearts race and our lives richer.

Life can throw curveballs, but love has the incredible ability to triumph over adversity. It's in the stories of individuals who faced hardships and yet found solace and strength in each other's arms. Love's resilience in the face of life's challenges is nothing short of inspiring.

Love is also a universal language, transcending borders and boundaries. The tales we've explored show us that love knows no cultural or geographical limits. It's a force that brings people from diverse backgrounds together, creating unique and beautiful connections.

Sometimes, love starts as friendship, a bond that deepens into something more profound. These stories remind us that the foundation of love often lies in the simple acts of kindness and support we offer to one another. It's a reminder of the profound impact friendship can have on our romantic lives.

And, of course, the tales of lasting love and commitment showcase the enduring power of love. They demonstrate that love, when nurtured and cherished, can withstand the tests of time and grow even stronger.

So, as we conclude this journey, let's celebrate the incredible beauty of love. It's not just the stuff of fairy tales; it's a force that enriches our lives in countless ways. It's a reminder that in the tapestry of our existence, love's threads weave some of the most beautiful and meaningful moments.